KELLY
THE RESCUE DOG

Tessa Krailing

Illustrated by Tony Morris

OXFORD
UNIVERSITY PRESS

OXFORD
UNIVERSITY PRESS

Great Clarendon Street, Oxford OX2 6DP

Oxford University Press is a department of the University of Oxford.
It furthers the University's objective of excellence in research, scholarship,
and education by publishing worldwide in

Oxford New York

Auckland Bangkok Buenos Aires Cape Town Chennai
Dar es Salaam Delhi Hong Kong Istanbul Karachi Kolkata
Kuala Lumpur Madrid Melbourne Mexico City Mumbai Nairobi
São Paulo Shanghai Taipei Tokyo Toronto

Oxford is a registered trade mark of Oxford University Press
in the UK and in certain other countries

British Library Cataloguing in Publication Data

Data available

ISBN 0 19 919 640 0

1 3 5 7 9 10 8 6 4 2

Mixed Pack (1 of 6 different titles): ISBN 0 19 919647 8
Class Pack (6 copies of 6 titles): ISBN 0 19 919646 X

Illustrated by Tony Morris c/o Linda Rogers
Associates and David Russell

Acknowledgements
pp4/5 Corel; p11 Sipa/Rex Features; p12 Simon Gillam;
p13 Simon Gillam; p15 Corel; p20 SIPA PRESS/Rex Features;
p27 Sipa/Rex Features; p10 Simon Gillam; p19 Sipa/Rex
Features; p45 Simon Gillam; p46 Simon Gillam;
pp46/47 Corel; p47 Simon Gillam.

Printed in China

Contents

Introduction

EARTHQUAKE ROCKS

Many Feared Buried Alive

On 17th August 1999, at 3 o'clock in the morning, a terrible earthquake shook western Turkey. It was one of the biggest earthquakes of the 20th century, measuring 7.4 on the **Richter Scale**.

It began with a low rumbling sound like thunder. Soon the rumbling grew into a roar. The ground shook and deep cracks opened up in the streets. Huge buildings collapsed, sending clouds of dust into the air. Within seconds the town of Izmit lay in ruins. Some people managed to escape and ran from their homes. Others were not so lucky.

During the next few hours rescue teams arrived from all over the world to help search for survivors of the earthquake. This story is about one such team from Britain and of a very special dog called Kelly.

WESTERN TURKEY

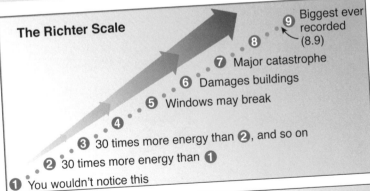

The Richter Scale

- **9** Biggest ever recorded (8.9)
- **8**
- **7** Major catastrophe
- **6** Damages buildings
- **5** Windows may break
- **4**
- **3** 30 times more energy than **2**, and so on
- **2** 30 times more energy than **1**
- **1** You wouldn't notice this

1

Buried Alive

"Dad," whispered Tariq. "Are you awake?"

Omar groaned and opened his eyes. "What's the matter, son?"

"I can't sleep," said Tariq. "It's too hot. I think there's a storm coming."

"You could be right," said Omar. "All day long it's felt like something is about to happen. Go back to bed, there's a good lad."

Tariq shook his head. "I'm going downstairs where it's cooler. Why don't you come with me?"

Omar yawned sleepily. "No, I think I'll stay here."

Tariq crept along the landing. He and his father were alone in the house. His mother and sister had gone to visit relatives in Ankara. He padded down the stairs to the kitchen and lay on the floor. The tiles were hard but beautifully cool. At last he fell asleep.

Suddenly he awoke with a start. In the distance he could hear a deafening roar, like thunder. It seemed to be coming closer and closer. The storm must have arrived, just as they expected.

But this was no ordinary storm. Within seconds the whole house began to shake. The china rattled and fell off the shelves with a crash. Tariq could feel the floor moving beneath him. What on earth was happening?

He jumped to his feet and tried to switch on the light. It didn't work. He started towards the back door, but just as he reached it there came a loud cracking noise. Next moment a pile of bricks came tumbling down around him. A terrible choking smell filled the air.

At last the dust cleared. Tariq was amazed to find that he was still alive. The framework of the doorway must have saved him. He called out, "Dad? Dad, are you all right?"

No answer.

*The earthquake at Izmit destroyed
many buildings and killed many people.*

Tariq stumbled back towards the
stairs – or rather, to where the stairs
used to be.

There was nothing left of them now
but a pile of rubble. A terrible fear took
hold of him. "Dad? Dad, where are
you?" he called again.

A strange, empty silence hung in the
air.

News of the earthquake spread quickly. In England Simon Gillam heard about it and started to pack. He packed a tent, a sleeping-bag, a cooking stove – and lots of dog food. Because Simon would not be travelling alone.

Volunteer Simon Gillam

Kelly is a Welsh Border Collie.

"Kelly! Kelly!" he called. "Come here, old girl. We've got work to do."

Kelly, a six-year-old **Border Collie**, came bounding up to him. Simon bent down to stroke her glossy head.

"This won't be an easy job," he warned her. "But we'll do our best – won't we, old girl?"

Kelly grinned up at him, eagerly
wagging her tail. She was a trained
search and rescue dog. Her job was to
find people buried beneath rubble or
mud. Together, she and Simon made a
brilliant team.

But it would be difficult, exhausting
work. And who knew what dangers
awaited them in the ruins of the
Turkish town?

2

The Magic Word

The pick-up truck lurched down the rough, uneven track and on to a smoother road. Kelly gazed out of the window. They had been travelling for hours and must be a long way from home. But she wasn't scared. She was never scared as long as she was with Simon.

Near the end of a long journey?

Kelly turned to look at Simon, squashed beside her in the back of the truck. He gave her a reassuring grin. "Won't be long now, old girl. Soon be there."

Soon be where?

Kelly could tell from his voice their journey was important. This wasn't going to be a holiday: they were here to work. But that suited her fine. There was nothing Kelly enjoyed more than working. Wherever they were going she couldn't wait to get there.

She had started her training when she was only a puppy. To her it was just a game of hide-and-seek. Simon would take her to a quarry or a building site and send one of his friends to hide. This friend took a squeaky toy with him. As soon as Kelly heard it go "Squeak, squeak!" she would rush off in search of the toy. When she had found it she barked to tell Simon how clever she was. Oh, it was a great game! Kelly loved playing hide-and-seek.

But now they had come to western
Turkey and it was no longer a game. She
wouldn't be searching for a squeaky toy.
She would be looking for real live
people in need of rescue.

The pick-up came to a sudden stop. "We're here," said Simon.

He opened the door and jumped out. Kelly followed him. Together they stood, looking at the ruined town. All they could see was a twisted mass of concrete and metal. It was hard to believe that people had once lived and worked in this place. Now it looked as if it had been flattened by a gigantic bomb.

The town of Izmit after the earthquake

20

The first thing they noticed was the heat. Although it was early morning it felt as if they were stepping into a warm oven. And there was a terrible smell in the air. Simon quickly grabbed his mask and pulled it over his face.

Kelly gazed up at him, wagging her tail. She was impatient to get started. But what did he want her to do?

"First we've got to find out where we're needed," he told her.

Already people were clambering towards them across the rubble. They had seen the pick-up truck arrive. Could it be someone who would help them find their missing friends or relations?

The first to reach them was a young boy. He grabbed Simon's arm, repeating the same word over and over again. "**Baba**, baba, baba."

"Sorry, I can't understand what you're saying." Simon looked over his shoulder at a man just getting out of the truck. "Ali! Over here – quick."

Ali was their **interpreter**. As soon as the boy realised Ali could speak Turkish he began to talk fast and urgently. Ali listened, sometimes nodding, sometimes shaking his head.

"What's he saying?" asked Simon.

"Baba is the Turkish word for 'father'," said Ali. "It seems the boy went to sleep downstairs, but his father stayed upstairs. Now he can't find him."

"Where's the house?" asked Simon.

Ali spoke to the boy, who pointed in the direction of the rubble. There was nothing left that looked like a house – or any other building. Was it possible that someone could still be alive under all that mess?

The boy grabbed Simon's arm again. "Baba," he said again. "Baba."

Simon turned to Ali. "What's the boy's name?"

"Tariq. He says his father's called Omar."

Simon nodded reassuringly at the boy. "Don't worry, Tariq. If your father's alive we'll find him."

Simon pulled a bright yellow jacket over Kelly's head. It had large letters on each side saying "RESCUE". The jacket told everyone that Kelly was a trained search and rescue dog with an important job to do. Finally he put little boots on her feet to protect them

Among such destruction could anyone still be alive?

from the hot stones.

All this told Kelly that the time had come for her to start work. She gazed up at Simon, waiting for him to say the magic word.

CHAPTER

3

A Game of Hide-and-Seek

"Find!" said Simon.

That was it! That was the magic word. Kelly set off quickly across the rubble. Light and sure-footed, she could search buildings that might collapse under the weight of a man. And she had a wonderful sense of smell. If a living person was buried beneath the rubble, Kelly would soon pick up the scent.

Simon followed her, holding on to a long line attached to her harness. "Careful, girl," he warned, giving the line a tug. "Not too fast."

Kelly slowed down. After a short distance she stopped and looked back at Simon, "Go on, girl," he said. "*Find!*"

Kelly gets to work

Kelly raised her head and sniffed the air. What did he want her to find? A person, of course. That's what this game of hide-and-seek was all about. But where should she look?

She sniffed again. This place was full of smells, most of them horrible. But there was only one smell she wanted to find – the scent of human breath. That would tell her there was someone still alive beneath the ruins. But it wouldn't be easy. It was never easy.

Simon watched her closely. He was waiting for her to start barking. That was the signal she was trained to give him if she found something. But Kelly did not bark. Instead she backed away from the place where she had been standing. No use wasting time there. No scent of human breath. She turned to the right and began again.

For twenty minutes she kept on searching. It was very hot. Soon her nose and eyes were coated with dust and she was panting hard. But she didn't give up. She never gave up until the game was over.

"Kelly, stop!" called Simon. "Time for a break. Come here."

Wearily she limped towards him. Simon shouted to the interpreter. "Ali! Can you find us a vehicle with air-conditioning? Kelly needs to cool down."

Ali found a **Range Rover** and told the driver to start up the engine. For ten minutes they sat inside, enjoying the chilled air. Soon Kelly began to recover. But they couldn't afford to rest for too long. Outside, the boy Tariq watched them with anxious eyes. He was waiting for them to continue the search. They climbed out of the vehicle and went back to the ruins.

Again Kelly set off across the rubble. She kept sniffing, her sharp nose seeking the faintest smell of a living body. Her tail never stopped wagging for an instant. Simon could see it waving like a flag. It told him she was still working – that she hadn't given up.

Suddenly she stopped, balanced on a pile of roof tiles. Her nose quivered.

What was that smell?

It was very faint... but yes, there it was again! There was definitely something there...

She peered down into the darkness, but she could see nothing. Nonetheless her nose told her that she was right. Something – no, some*one* – was lying in the tangled mass of concrete below her. And they were breathing, whoever they were.

The game of hide-and-seek was over. She had found what she was looking for – a living person. Oh, she couldn't wait to tell Simon! She must give him the signal straight away.

Kelly raised her head and barked.

Rescue!

Lying beneath the rubble, Omar heard
the barking. He opened his eyes and
listened. It must be a stray dog, looking
for food in the ruins. Once or twice he
thought he heard Tariq's voice, but he
hadn't the strength to reply. A heavy
weight lay across his legs, making it
impossible to move. He didn't know
how long he had been lying here. It
seemed like days. He had almost given
up hope.

The dog barked again. Omar moistened his lips. He shouted in a cracked voice, "Help! Help, I'm down here!"

A man's voice called out something in a language he didn't understand. Soon afterwards he heard noises above his head – alarming noises of earth and **masonry** being shifted. It sounded as if they were using some kind of heavy lifting gear. Omar closed his eyes, afraid that more rubble would fall on top of him.

Great care must be taken when shifting bricks and stones as a building might collapse further

Then, suddenly, he saw daylight. Faces peered in at him. Someone spoke in Turkish: "Keep still. We'll soon have you out of there."

At last the heavy weight was lifted off his legs. But he couldn't move them. He seemed to have lost all feeling.

Slowly, carefully, Omar was lifted out and laid on a **stretcher**. The pain was so great that he almost fainted, but then he heard his son's voice: "Dad! Dad, don't worry – you're safe now. They're taking you to the hospital."

He opened his eyes. "Hello, Tariq," he said weakly.

"It was the dog who found you," Tariq told him. "It saved your life."

Omar could make no sense of it. He felt tired and confused. "Your mother will be worried..."

"I'll let her know we're okay. I'll send a message by radio," Tariq promised.

"Good boy." Omar gripped his son's hand.

As they lifted him into the ambulance he caught sight of a dog wearing a bright yellow jacket. Funny, he had never really liked dogs much. How strange that one should have saved his life...

Wearily he closed his eyes as the ambulance drove him away.

Kelly was exhausted and covered with a thick grey dust. Simon took her to a nearby water tanker and hosed her down with clear, cold water. She shook herself furiously, splashing Simon all over. But he didn't mind getting wet. He was just relieved that she was safe.

"Well done, old girl," he said. "I'm very, very proud of you."

Kelly gazed up at him, wagging her tail. She felt proud, too. After all, she had played her favourite game – and won!

Simon and Kelly – the Rescue Dog

Story Background

This story is based on an actual rescue. Tariq is not a real character, but what happened to him is typical of the rescues carried out by RAPID UK.

Simon and Kelly are very real, as you can see from the photograph. They both worked for RAPID UK, an emergency rescue charity. RAPID UK is based in the United Kingdom but there are offices in other parts of the world.

Simon and Kelly at work

Gemma and Kelly are both search and rescue dogs.

Sadly, rescue dogs must go into **quarantine** for six months on their return to the UK. The Passports for Pets scheme does not cover those areas outside Europe where RAPID UK most often has to work.

If you want to find out more about RAPID UK, you can visit their website: **www.rapidsar.org.uk**

Note from Publisher: the author has chosen to donate her fee and royalties from this book to RAPID UK

Index

Glossary

Baba the Turkish word for father

Border Collie breed of sheep-dog with long hair, pointed nose, and bushy tail

interpreter person who translates orally from one language to another

masonry building material, usually stonework

quarantine period of time when person or animal has to be kept in isolation to prevent contagious diseases from spreading

Range Rover large vehicle which can travel over rough ground

Richter Scale measurement of force of an earthquake. The higher the number the worse the earthquake

stretcher frame with handles for carrying sick or injured person